# FLYIl
# UNDERWATER

# *Flying Underwater*

Anna Adams

**PETERLOO POETS**

First published in 2004
by Peterloo Poets
The Old Chapel, Sand Lane, Calstock, Cornwall PL18 9QX, U.K.

© 2004 by Anna Adams

The moral rights of the author are asserted in accordance with the Copyright, Designs and Patent Act, 1988

All rights reserved. No part of this publication may be reproduced, stored in a retrieval system, or transmitted, in any form or by any means, electronic, mechanical, photocopying, recording or otherwise without the prior permission in writing of the publisher.

**A catalogue record for this book is available from the British Library**

**ISBN 1-904324-12-6**

Printed in Great Britain By
Antony Rowe Ltd, Chippenham, Wilts.

# ACKNOWLEDGEMENTS

Acknowledgements are due to the following publications in which some of these poems made their first appearance:

*Acumen, The Craven Heritage Journal, The Dalesman, The Green Book, The Interpreter's House, The London Magazine, News From Somewhere, The North, Pennine Platform, Poetry London, Poetry Review, The Rialto, Scintilla, Spokes, Stand, Thames Guardian,* and *The Yorkshire Journal.*

Three poems, "The Outdoor Room", "Genius Loci" and "Orion in September", were included among the New Poems in *Green Resistance*, a book of Selected and New Poems from Enitharmon in 1996, and "The River Goddess in the A to Z" was included in a *Something Understood* programme on Radio 4 in 2002.

Thanks are also due to James Harpur for sharp-eyed help with the proof-reading, and for one or two stolen ideas.

# Contents

Page

| | |
|---|---|
| 9 | The River Goddess in the A to Z |
| 11 | Crossing Hungerford Bridge |
| 12 | View of Waterloo Bridge from Hungerford Bridge |
| 13 | Cormorants Diving |
| 14 | The Song of the Beggar's Child |
| 15 | To Bede's Sparrow |
| 16 | Jizz |
| 17 | Hawthorn Hedges |
| 18 | At Midwinter |
| 20 | The Tems |
| 21 | Monologue of the Retired Fishing Bailiff – i.m. M.T. |
| 23 | The Wood Along the River's Bank |
| 25 | Memorials |
| 29 | Family Grove |
| 31 | Orion in September: A Journey Home |
| 33 | Stolen Moon Fragments – 6 haiku |
| 34 | The Outdoor room |
| 36 | Genius loci |
| 38 | Two Robins in One Garden |
| 39 | Love Poem |
| 41 | Arrival of the Swifts |
| 43 | Garden Spiders in October |
| 44 | By Robin Light |
| 45 | Brownfield Building Site |
| 47 | The Chorus |
| 48 | Heart Murmur |
| 49 | October Leafsong |
| 51 | Miss Jones |
| 53 | Thomas de Quincey, Down and Out in London |
| 54 | Hölderlin's Last Night |
| 55 | The Sofa |

| | |
|---|---|
| 58 | Millennial Funerals |
| 63 | Filling in the Form |
| 66 | The Angel |
| 67 | The Crimson Rose |
| 68 | Knocking On |

## *The River Goddess in the A to Z*

Blue contours of a living limb,
full curves suggesting hip and breast
abutting on right-angled, ruled
geometry of streets,
are fragments of the undivided
river-body, serpent soul
of London, sliding past the ranks
of buildings on both river banks.

Reclined at ease, reflecting skies
far deeper than her bed, inhaling tides
brackish with North Sea salt, exhaling them
twice daily, dwindling then to puny size,
she knows in every molecule
of tributaries, river-mist, grey rain
and snowflakes vanishing in leaden skin
that she's an international local thing.

She makes her bed as she lies restlessly
on gravel; and, though British born,
she's an illegal immigrant. She's come
by cloud from Amazonian and African
and Asian waters. She has flown
to both the poles, circled the world's wide waist,
and is more cosmopolitan
than the great town she jigsaws, mirrors, joins.

There should be wisdom in her, reconciling
all that she knows with all that she has been:
rainforest, icefloe, flesh. If I look deep
and long into this liquid-muscled snake–
barred in by twenty bridges, who escapes
continuously–will my scale-dazzled eyes

see past her temporary local form
into her holy permanence? For she

led the procession that the earliest city
assembled on both banks to watch go by.
She mystifies the river-bordering park,
and is the wilderness at large in town,
stalking voluptuously by measured streets,
wearing the seamless sari of the world
dyed in our northern skies. She's grey and old,
gold and immortal: not to be controlled.

## *Crossing Hungerford Bridge*

At either end of Hungerford's long frieze
of walkers crossing Thames with scissor legs,
reclining figures, draped in blankets, pose
as sculpture: statues with a hand that begs.
The first prompts me to grope for silver pieces
while I stand still and let my heart slow down
after too many stairs. The flood tide rises
and bears gifts to the richer end of town.
Midway, an old man flutes an Irish jig
in payment for our payment, if we pay;
the statue at the far end, with a dog,
accepts my toll, and I go on my way
the richer, every time I walk this plank,
for more complacency stashed in the bank.

## *View of Waterloo Bridge*

Over the river in five easy leaps
the concrete hurdler, like a skimming stone,
bounces four times on water, striking roots
that grow into a bridge: a mantel-shelf
of ornaments and trophies, wedding-cakes,
cheese-graters, a dome-lidded biscuit tin,
and clockwork mice that glide along the edge.
Two hours transform these things to mystery.

Now, dim in misty dusk, the great dome seems
remote as god, while floodlights show St. Bride's
as child among vast, faintly printed tombs
that hint at life within; below, ebb tide –
combed by the bridges – coiling through the City –
races from Richmond to the estuary.

## *Cormorants Diving*

Twin cormorants at swim, which means 'at dive',
    meet only intermittently above
the roof of their cool pantry where, alive,
    they store bright shoals of minnows in the grove
of river-weeds that wave upstream or down
    according to the ebbing/flowing tide.
They take no interest in land-bound man;
    their world is river-shaped, more long than wide,
and only river-deep. They use the sky
    for ritual mating flights, and are well schooled
in bird deportment, tilting small chins high,
    and grooming, keeping plumage preened and oiled.

But their true beings' bliss, their bodies' thought,
is flying underwater, out of sight.

## *The Song of the Beggar's Child*

I lie across my mother's knees
and people tall as walking trees
look down upon me as I lie
and look away and hurry by.

I lie across my mother's lap;
her brown hand shakes the money-cup.
Men hear its rattled lullaby
and hurriedly they walk away.

The jangly music money makes
sings bread and soup, potato-cakes
and shelter from the rainy sky.
Men duck their heads and hurry by.

They keep the coins that are the key
to happiness: sweet mugs of tea
and freedom to stand up and play:
but hurriedly they walk away.

I learn my mother's trade. I whine –
"We have no country of our own:
no house, no bed; please Sir –" I say
the English words. They walk away

weighed down by pockets in their coats,
chocful of money, even notes
whose magic signs could set us free
to leave this pitch and walk away.

I long to find the money-mill,
the money-tree, the money-hill
or well, the bottomless supply
that packs the purses that pass by.

## *To Bede's Sparrow*

No, little spark, naive mistaken Sparrow,
this is no banquet hall you've blundered into:
it is the storm itself. You are its eye,
and have too much to do avoiding birdshot,
finding scraps to eat and flying straight
in force-nine gales of passion, terror, sorrow –
that sweep you right off course in Time's great tent –
ever to get your bearings, or remember
the fault you entered by, or why you came
into confusion from the simple light.

The tent-pole bends, almost to breaking-point;
the canvas flaps like gunfire, rain sprays in
through perforations in our starry roof.
The great thanes' banquet is for cannibals,
so all who eat are eaten, course by course.
If sparrrowhawks, or cruel men, or cats
don't get you, worms will win, for change is law.
The password in Time's kingdom is Goodbye –
to eggs and siblings, sparrow-chatter, feasts
and gutter-fights, and slummy sparrow-nests.

Imagine, little spark, a sunless moorland
stretching, featureless, to dim horizons;
and, hovering over one bogwater pool,
a furious swarm of midges. That is Time.
Or else, think of a desert without limits,
and – lost in it – a city like Las Vegas:
shrill with sirens, bright with flashing lights,
with no roads out but no walls round it either:
its people have no wish to go exploring,
unlike invading sand on desert winds.

# *Jizz*

1.
Bird-watchers have a necessary word
for distant silhouettes, the shape and stance
of grounded lapwings, or that war-lord bird
the kestrel, and the dipper's curtsey-dance
on mossy midstream stones; or – over wide
and tidal Thames – the motionless, erect
grey cipher that means heron at his trade.
For, at a glance, bird-watchers can detect
a species, and their secret is the "jizz",
which word is neither Norse nor Latinate,
and has no truck with Greek and all that jazz.
It was forged out of need to indicate
the jizz, explained above, which all things have:
birds, foxes, hares, and trees; and men I love.

2.
Trees have it, so we know them at a look –
if we know them at all – from moving cars,
and recognise an ash, a beech, an oak,
not by the details: leaf shape, dangling keys,
red haze of poplar catkins, leafy shelves
of pink-and-white confections, shedding snow;
or acorns, beechmast, pinecones. Bristling selves,
by their defiant jizz, are what we know;
and jizz expresses joy though lacking leaves.
So dreary winter's naked armatures –
the bones well-covered summer hid in sleeves –
are not in mourning while each tree endures
the saturated dark, but, full of fight,
distilleries of green wait on the light.

## *Hawthorn Hedges*

(for the shade of John Clare who planted some of them.)

The sweet come-hither chorus lines of Summer –
lacy as frothing waves at ocean's edges –
now play the tragedy of deep Midwinter:
long files of refugees freeze in the hedges.

Poor vagrant Queens, dim grey in frosty dawn,
shine white till risen sunrays melt them red;
each sheds her ermine for a bloodstained gown,
then offers her crown-jewels with bowed head.

The Mayflower Gaieties kept open house
for minstrels, beckoning with budding wands
which turned to blessings the forgiven curse
of boundaries that stole our common lands;
but, penitent in Winter, give their blood
to keep the shows of Summer on the road.

## *At Midwinter*

i.m. Ted Hughes

Where two stone bridges handcuff two wild streams –
Brants Ghyll and the Ribble – in dark hoops,
their waters merge to one hush-hushing river.
I watch while cold rain slants on the northwest wind.
Moss-black boulders hump out of the current,
enduring it as I endure the wind
that numbs my bare, umbrella-gripping hand
as I stand staring till the sliding world
of water washing stones by sleeping trees
appears entirely mineral.

I see the corpse of nature, scenery
without a play, without a genius
writing his fluent script with no line marred
as Shakespeare wrote to animate the Globe.
I don't feel disappointed, since I came
for respite from indoors, and hoped for nothing
but this conveyor-belt of nothingness.
And so I stand and wait, expecting nothing
and no-one, till I have become
at one with Winter.

Then sudden, through the river-bridge, arrives
a fire-blue missile, low and purposeful.
It flies, then pauses, perches on a stone
and is the Kingfisher – that morpho-blue,
metallic, tropical/exotic bird
that flits along Greek shores, whose range extends
southeast, all down the Ganges, and – unchanged –
is common near Calcutta, and beyond.
And yet, in summer silk, it toughs it out
all year on Yorkshire becks.

Condensed from rivers, hatched in fishbone nests
from pebble eggs, it's fed on fish until
skin-splinters sprout as quills all sheathed in silver.
Full fledged, it's blue as river-swallowed sky
seen through the leafy archway underwater,
and orange as reflected sunset-fire.
This bright untouchable – no creature eats it –
sees me, takes flight and dwindles to a spark:
a shot of joy that vanishes downriver,
turning the winter's corner.

## *The Tems*

Tems Beck streams through Giggleswick,
    circulating Earth's cool blood:
water seemingly less thick
    than London's khaki flood
though related to great Thames
    close as Smith to Smythe; its name
differs, but not so its genes.
    Warm it up, Tems' water steams.

Buckhaw Brow to Gildersleets:
    two miles long and two feet deep,
navigable by duck fleets,
    fordable by rural jeep.
Tems has been hemmed in of late;
    bridges link its grassy banks:
some are huge flat slabs of slate,
    some are arches, some are planks.

Wild as Thames and tame as Thames,
    little Tems's dozen bridges
carry mazy village lanes
    south of Craven's craggy ridges
where, before she knew her name,
    unformed England broke her spine:
sea-laid limestone bedding-planes
    slipped and shifted out of line.

That is where the lesser Tems –
    streaming past low drystone walls
hung with wild geraniums –
    dreams of raining on St. Paul's.

# *Monologue of the retired Fishing Bailiff*

(i.m. Mark Thompson)

Don't talk to me of books: I never read one.
I learn things manually, you know,
he said, twisting his fingers. I don't read,
nor watch the television. If I can't
see things wi' my own eyes I do wi'out.
Nay, books has never been much use to me;
nor newspapers; nor holidays. My wife
insisted, once, and she arranged it all:
a holiday at Morcambe for us both.
What's this? I said, when she packed up my clothes.
We tek the train to Morcambe in the morning.
We never do, I said. We do, she said,
and she were right. She'd booked a week in lodgings.
I couldn't tek to it. It weren't for me;
so I went out next morning, after breakfast,
and saw a bus to Hornby, and I took it,
then walked to Kirkby Lonsdale, got a lift
to Ingleton, but missed the evening bus
so I walked home by moonlight. I were tired
but happier wi' every step I took.
When I got in, Police was at the door:
Your wife raised the alarm; thought you was lost.
I was, but I'm not now, I said; Not now.
So after that she took the holidays,
and even went abroad, but I stop home.

I know the river, Ribblehead to Settle;
I know the becks, I know the roads and lanes –
for wasn't I the roadman once? – I know
the Tarn, and all the folk about the valley,
and many in yon graveyard. I remember
the man who built the walls on yonder fell.
He worked alone, for years, out on the mountain

with sheep and hares and skylarks, and the kestrel.
And he could read the sky, and so can I,
And I can read the ground and learn the news
of mushrooms, mink, and when the Osprey comes.
I can read well enough, but not in books.
Don't talk to me of books. Tell me you've seen
the kingfisher, or tell me that the otters
have took up residence wi' us again.

## *The Wood along the River's Bank*

(for Father Denis Clinch)

This is the church where nature prays
while, ceaselessly whispering rosaries,
the rock-bottom river of boulder-beads
creeps under mossed root buttresses.

This is the water, gold as wine,
of the river whispering rosaries
that feeds the roots of the tiptoe trees
supporting lofty canopies
that shade the church where nature prays.

And these are the cloisters in washed-out roots
where church-mice wrens can meditate
on insect-game and nesting-site
or chant Hail Maries, lost in light,
high in the perpendicular choir
of the church where nature prays.

And this is the secular farmer's field
where tractors mow the embroidered grass
of midsummer's vestments, and swallows, filled
with insects bred in the meadow's hide,
go sip the river of holy wine
or chase in the airy chapel's cage
through broken windows of foliage.

And these are the votive candles, set
on the shadowy floor, giving flame-blue light
from luminous flowers along the route
of the river of heavenly reveries
where bluecoat swallows skim deep trout-pools
and – twittering like a Sunday-school

in navy jackets with earwig tails –
they perch in rows along altar rails.

And seed is the answer to nature's prayer:
full as a bible with holy words
to spell out buds and fledgeling birds
and luminous campaniles of flower
spread by autumn's replenishing floods
that furnish the sacred riverside grove –
choir, clerestorey, aisle and nave –
with incense, anthem and altar fire
for the church where nature prays.

But where is the builder, Jack-in-the-Green?
He dies in winter to rise in spring
and haunt live pillars whose leafy crowns
mask shining eyes that watch unseen
the visiting swallow and resident wren,
and lonely riverside-walking man.
He senses the gaze of unblinking Jack
conning his tattered and torn heart's book
and the burden that bows his back,
in the church where nature prays.

## *Memorials*

1. THE REDSTARTS

Summer's redstarts haunt the mossgrown ashtrees;
russet tail-fans, darting through the spaces
between moss-green and green, wake memory
that switches on internalised recordings.
"A robin with the red slipped round its tail"
I hear my father's voice, his hint of cockney.
"The rusty coloured tail is what you notice."
Since he fell silent our shy summer redstarts
are his memorial

and living monuments to unremembered
ancestors that shared their redstart summers
between the moss-green ashtrees and the rowans –
whose berries, in their progress toward scarlet,
match the redstart's tail for one day's moment.
Thirty generations of these migrants
must have homed in above my five-barred gate
discounting time that strings the beads of summer
in endless necklaces.

My father, in the summer of my life
when I had little children – lines of nappies
strung between the ashes and the rowans –
pointed out the redstarts and the skylark
singing above our field. But then I had
little time for birds, since I was rearing
nestlings of my own, and worked as hard
as they did, almost, blindly laying down
memorials to myself.

My mother too has her memorials:
the cherrytree we planted when she died
has daughters, sapling-slender lissom daughters
and daughters of those daughters. Memories
themselves turn into memories, more blurred
with every printing. But her tree's a grove
of cherrytrees – all valid as the first –
as are this summer's redstarts, wheatears, dippers,
named by a distant voice.

She also had a voice – I echo it –
but I inherited, then lost, her box
of coloured cotton bobbins, bias bindings,
thimble, graded needles, random buttons,
spare elastic: implements for mending.
To lift the lid released my mother's genie –
the scent of home, her kitchen's crimson tiles
and shabby lino. Quarrels. Shrill tirades,
and her heroic silence.

2. SAILING BY

Half-past-midnight's music, "Sailing By"
heralds the weather-warnings for trawlermen,
yachtsmen, tankers, lonely ocean-rowers
pondskating over unmapped water-dunes
in areas like Rockall, German Bight.
Then "Coastal waters" traces a top-heavy chart
of squat, square-headed Britain, sitting hard
on Kent and Sussex, hatching the Isle of Wight,
bathing its Cornish feet in Atlantic suds
and hugging Wales to its narrow chest, while Ireland
swims away to the West.

I could chant a limited personal list
of seaside stations: Selsey Bill, Southend,
Felixstowe, Sutton-on-Sea, St. Margaret's Bay;
then Leiston, Filey, Swanage, Lulworth Cove –
to map my childhood summers.
War was hiatus. Bardsey, Lindisfarne,
then Inishmore, and Scarp in the Hebrides
where I first heard that music – "Sailing By" –
as I enjoyed my late-night fireside bath
while southwest gales rocked house and boat and bay
and all the rest to sleep.

The Hebrides are twenty years away
but that unchanging half-past-midnight tune
still makes our long-abandoned sheiling rise
around me and enclose me, instantly.
Soft tilley-lamplight shows me wooden walls –
tongued and grooved – the painted vertical grain
rivering upward, swerving round dead-wood eyes.
Our looted, or else beachcombed, bric-a-brac –
flat-irons, gannet-skulls, wild flowers in jars
crowd the shelf above the stove
backed by the pinned-up map of Scotland's rocks.

Juniper Horizontalis's rickety bones –
twisted by wind – sprawl on the dresser-top.
Above, on a shelf, four blue enamel plates
Like portholes, and – of utilitarian beauty –
four thick white army-surplus porage bowls.
In a drawer, my inherited tin of needles and thread,
scissors and suchlike, holds my mother's ghost –
imprisoned air of home – and on the walls
paintings of sea, and mountains in the sea,
and one of an ultramarine and scarlet lobster
such as my sons braved drowning for, most mornings.

The sisal matting filters white sea-sand,
not dust, and the dying fire would smell of peat,
not coal, if it hadn't gone out; and the stripe of light
beneath the bedroom door has gone out too
with a sigh from the pressure lamp, as "Sailing By"
sailed by and arrived at silence.
The phantom house collapses along with the island,
sinking fathoms down in the foaming sea,
drowning my mother's old tin with her mending-gear
decades deep in the past. Unreachable, now,
is the coffined air that used to transport me home.

## *Family Grove*

Beneath my shadowy father-tree
    small rain leaks through the leaves;
his blossom is promises, promises, and
    a chill wind grieves.

Beneath my shadowy mother-tree,
    laden with acid fruits,
gusts of rage shake down the leaves
    that fall on broken roots.

Within my own self's shadow-tree
    I shelter in tough bark,
and grow a secret shadow-root
    across time's hollow dark

beneath the two great Worldwide Wars
    that killed so many men
they hid in huge and general pain
    small pains of nineteen-ten

like the death of my child-father's mother
    and that of my child-mother's dad,
and that of her seven-year sister
    which drove their mother mad.

    Here lies small Auntie Doris,
        here lie her slender bones,
    shut in the dark like a shot-down lark
        crushed under earth and stones.

    So weep for wasted blossom,
        and weep for blasted fruit:
    childbirth, TB, diptheria
        and damaged heart and root.

      Dead dolls lay in the parlour
          with curtains drawn all day;
   the undertakers' horsedrawn hearse
       carried childhood away.

Yet the blossoming tree of our father
    and our mother's burdened tree
made a threadbare tent in the Thirties
    shelter enough for three:

so forgive, forgive their failures;
    wonder at their success;
with every excuse for reproaches
    their shadowy trees still bless.

## *Orion in September*

(a journey home)

Above the car park, bright as diamonds,
Orion leaping in the southern dark
from midnight to extinction in the sun
was my last souvenir, found as we left
one hour before the dawn.

We drove out of the Midi: crossed the Rhone
and crawled by hairpin bends to that high plain
where, white as marble statues on the green,
calm tribes of cattle graze. They sit or stand
like warm and breathing stone.

Still carrying my gift, Orion's brooch,
inside my head, I came to Vézelay
where on his tympanum, high out of reach,
a Christ in Glory spreads out giant hands
to give his light away.

A supernatural wind blows through the stone
and animates the saints; their draperies
are dancing though their limbs are sitting down,
and like a sea alive with vortices
is the Lord Jesus's gown.

I think of those tumultuous night skies
that Vincent caught in whirlpools of blue marks.
He longed to reach the stars. His piercing eyes
saw them as more than matter, or mere sparks,
but heavenly destinies,

though he did not believe. Awestruck Anon,
eight hundred years before, gazing by night,
saw that vast firefly dance. Between each one

he joined the dots to make a Man of Light
who heard the prayers of men.

Stars answer eyes and eyes reflect the stars;
a great Sky Father swings across the deep
reflected in our minds. His bright trapeze –
Orion's belted quadrilateral –
glitters throughout our sleep.

## *Stolen Moon Fragments: 6 haiku*

Nineteen sixty nine:
we see on television
the first Moonlanding.

Stolen moon fragments –
dark as barbados sugar –
lie in museums.

We call it "mooning" –
baring bent-over bottoms –
but Moon is no bum.

We see no footprints
in spite of Man's moon-trespass.
Moon is self cleansing

and is as silver,
aloof and pale and polished
as ever, from Earth.

How extravagant
or lunatic to go there
just to say we'd been.

## *The Outdoor Room*

Walls on three sides, with windows into shadow,
shelter my tiny but tree-furnished garden,
and, closing up this alcove, a high fence
dams back the sunrise, keeps a reservoir
of morning dazzle on its eastern side
until it spills and splashes through tree branches
onto the parquet of my brick-paved room.
And to this space, this small suburban space,
the universe comes visiting each day.
And to these days, this summer day, this now,
comes history, coiled in its hiding place;
not even ignorance can keep us safe.

I need not know what lies beyond the fence.
There's nothing of much moment: other gardens,
alleyways, a carpark. Crashing glass
means the well-meaning bottlebank. The traffic
growling westward, goes to Somerset,
and the embankment to the south of us
supports both District Line and Piccadilly –
now overground and racing to Heathrow.
The river's curve, beyond the Chiswick High Road,
defines this area, shaped like an udder
hung on the old Bath Road. Above its map
grey jets glance down on nowhere of importance.

Thin clouds obscure the aircraft: slow grey fish
drift overhead, changing at night to dragons
with emeralds and rubies in their tails.
The moon is caught and cullised in the baytree
that struggles with the gale beyond the wall:
it reassembles, free, above the roofridge,
to stare, amazedly, into my garden.
Here we are mortal, everything is mortal

and therefore of great worth. I never know
what treasure may be tossed over the fence:
the moon, a ball, small birds, the raucous jay,
or bruising apples dropped by our own tree.

In early Spring, the quince wears muted scarlet
petals the colour of the silk pyjamas
my father gave my mother in the Thirties,
hoping the ardent colour might warm up
her frightened sexuality.
I could unlock my childhood with such keys.
Now polka-dots of appleblossom petals
pattern the mossy ground. If this were all –
this ragged butterfly, that sievelike ceiling –
this outdoor room could be the needle's eye
for all experience to be dragged through.
Its insignificance would be enough.

## *Genius Loci*

The vendor gave no warning, naturally.
We went to view his house; he showed it to us;
he wasn't offering his next-door neighbour.
So when we came with keys, to take possession,
Emmeline surprised us.
She leant out from what should have been a roof
and said Don't buy it, don't buy it from him.
We have already bought it, we replied.
Then, from the walltop, she poured grievances:
told us that he had tried to steal her garden,
blocked her view with fences, stolen light.
And then she had been firebombed, so she said,
by would-be property developers.
But she stayed on, under her broken roof
and the bay-laurel planted at her birth,
grown up to a green tenement of birds.

One summer day she paid a formal call,
wearing a long white dress, a big straw hat
draped with a chiffon scarf, and cotton gloves.
She sipped a glass of water, and confided:
Before the fire my second husband paid
the rent. I could not pay Electric Bills.
I simply do not know how one makes money.
After the fire she wouldn't move away
but camped among the ruins, sifting ash.
She sorted her charred sketchbooks, covered up,
with plastic sheeting, sculpture by her father
whose workshop it had been. I am, she said,
the Last Indigenous Chiswickian.
It may have been her candles fired the place,
but in those greedy years the site alone,
of her old studio, was worth a bomb.

She comes and goes in Winter, comes to stay
in Summertime; sits under her Bay-laurel
teaching her grand-daughter to read and count.
She reared four children. Most Important Work,
she said when she called round, and I concurred.
She moved me, but won't speak to me these days
because I said she might have squatters' rights
to fight the machinations of the Council.
She took offence, thinking I meant to mean
the Last Indigenous Chiswickian –
who grew here – was a squatter.
I should have called it "negative possession".

One freezing day she climbed the hidden ladder
and leant out from what should have been a roof
to stare reproachfully at my dark windows.
I was no better than the other upstarts
who think they own the Earth.
If she forgives me I would like to tell her
that flickering candle-light and drifting woodsmoke –
meaning she has come home by bicycle
and climbed the carpark fence into her garden,
scorning Chubb locks, security alarms
and all our title deeds – can soothe my sense
of exile from the outgrown place she keeps.

## *Two Robins in One Garden*

They give no warning, but arrive
like blobs of shadow tossed over the fence
out of a wintry world into our yard.
First one, and then its fellow, drop, touch down
and bounce about, concerned
only with studying the crevices
between the bricks that herringbone our ground.
Neither ever comes without the other
to peck my scattered crumbs or stab at worms
and shake them, like red-breasted terriers.
Might they be twins, hatched from one crowded egg
and linked, thereafter, by one robin-soul?
They show such tact, they are so circumspect,
they never glare, full frontal, each at each,
with ruffled waistcoats blazing for a fight,
but look askance, half-turning olive backs,
like naked girls embarrassed by their chests,
hiding aggressive vests, suggesting Pax,
though they switch their red traffic-lights on me –
the giant who dug the ground and scattered crumbs –
which is quite brave of them. It gives me comfort
that these two siblings or, it may be, spouses,
should break the rules of war and keep the peace,
holding their fire and sharing one small garden;
thus contradicting custom. If mere robins
can do it, so can we.

## *Love Poem*

Someone or something has at last switched off
the great outdoor refrigerator. Frost
relents, and air turns gentle. All night long
earth-washing rain fell perpendicular,
and penetrated cracks in paving stones
to comfort roots and waken lust in worms.

This morning, on our brick-paved yard,
one couple lies outstretched, still copulating
as such hermaphroditic creatures do
after their fashion.
They lie as parallel as railway-lines,
but closer, each one's tail still poking down
earth's exit, so it can
retreat at once, if need be: but not yet.

This long encounter measures fourteen inches –
worms are too elastic to be metric –
and bleached bloodless, pale as string,
but for the swollen saddles, kissing-close
and rosy as though wounded, but they are
made healthy by the illness we call "love"
and it appears to be as sweet to them –
or sweeter – as to that pair of Verona.

Blind to dawn, and deaf to nightingales
or larks, and unafraid of god or man,
they know the consummation that they dreamed
shut up all winter in the frozen convent
till water beckoned them up to the air;
and they know nothing else.

Their food is dust drawn in by lipless mouths,
if we can call them mouths; and earthworm clothes
are nakedness of nakedness: they're stripped
to gut – an independent inner tube
spined by a core of mud.
It's certain that they hold no conversation,
and lack all matter for it, in no brain.
Worm-talk is silence, groping with no limbs
in unadulterated innocence
for that first word that whispered down
the crumbling stairs of earth, and made them climb.

## *Arrival of the Swifts*

Late afternoon, something impelled me out
into our small backyard to watch the sky.

Where one small pickaxe shadow, one dark swift
had cut across the rooftops yesterday
a score of them was interweaving flightpaths
above my shady rectangle of ground.

Shrieking like blackboard chalks that mark the air
with a cat's-cradle of self-healing cuts,
birds flapped to overtake, rode pickaback,
so two became one bird with four curved wings
and proved this party was an airborne wedding.

After their journey from the Southern Cape,
swifts need no touchdown on the solid earth.
Their feet are not for walking, even perching.
Tireless as healthy hearts they work their wings
till death, but for their annual sitting-in
to brood on two white eggs: but even then

the swifts would hang their cradles on the air
and rear their young between treetops and cirrus
or in the bellies of white vapour-whales
were winds reliable, for, though unstable,
wild air provides the flotsam furnishings
of nursery footholds: gives them stolen goods

such as – grass wisps, straw shreds, leaf skeletons,
dandelion seeds flown far from home,
hair-combings, ravelled wool, discarded feathers
that might drift in the currents of the air
forever, did swift-sweepers not recover
and spittle-glue them to some ledge or crevice.

Such are their bivouacs: mere collages
of wind-wrack; and their food
is atmospheric plankton, insect swarms
bred in the disregarded habitats
below, concealed by the indifference
of migrant specialists who see a map:

and yet, for all their lifestyle, they're not angels
nor more etherial than mudpie martins,
(for air is as material as earth)
though Gabriel swifts bring blessings, their glad tidings –
Summer's annunciation.

## *Garden Spiders in October*

Invisible as angels, or as air,
they hang designedly unseen
until, slanting between
house walls, sundown illuminates
silk targets huge as giant dinner plates.

Like ghosts, they shiningly appear
ragged with shadow-holes that still
deceive some prey, though full
of small gold leaves and silver dust,
and skeletons from the air-fishers' feast.

Vertical labyrinths whose minotaurs
in miniature cling on –
big-bellied, upsidedown –
to straws in summer's plughole, drowning in
engulfing vortices round haloed skulls.

## *By Robin Light*

(Newcastle upon Tyne)

Earth gets in its own light
soon after noon; my garden
is sunken deep in shade
as I dig in the sodden
molasses-sticky clay
that clogs my levering spade.

To sort seedling from weed
is hazardous in darkness
while cataracts of shadow
are rushing down the vortex
of deep midwinter's throat:
but earth's fire is not out.

An animated ember –
last spark of rosy summer
still glowing in December –
flits silently about
and reassures the gloom
that summer will rekindle from its flame.

## *Brownfield Building Site*

Elbow-necked and caterpillar-tracked,
metallic dinosaurs attack
and excavate cars' tarmac habitat.
They peck with shovel-beaks
and swivel on their bases, dropping soil
in spoil-heaps on the site.

Trenches exhale stale breath
of the polluted brook, piped up and buried
where once it purled through water-meadows.
Then came the railway-sidings and their coalyard,
bordered with allotments, till the car
displaced the railway, covered all with carpark.

Now it is transformation-time again.
The blackened earth itself is Lazarus –
full of immortal seed. The sun
already warms it. A revolving urn
of liquid walls pours out grey concrete-slides
into the empty tombs, to be foundations

for human homes. And here a bounding wall
stands six foot tall with some authority,
while rectangles – dry paddling-pools with drains
and doorway-gaps in place – map out new dwellings.
Each weekday the controlling men clock in
to puppeteer the waltzing slave-machines.

Sunshine persuades hard-hatted men to strip,
and slowly cooks their pasty torsos pink
then brown, with buttock-cleavages on show.
And over fences scribbled with graffiti,
magnolias drop litter while the cherry
and pear trees blossom into peaks of snow;

and soon the risen walls wear roofs,
and planks lie down as floors. Through painted doors
enter new families whose dreaming children
will think their houses have existed always,
to last forever, till time teaches them
to sense, beneath their home, the tainted stream.

## *The Chorus*

The neutral voice of News
speaks of another massacre
in Africa. A witness
tells of what he saw:

three armoured trucks arrived,
stopped in the village square –
armed men jumped down, ran everywhere –
rounded up men and boys ...

Clear, beyond the witness,
I heard the green savannah:
bird-flutes and sighing trees,
deep gasps and monkey-cries,

and thought: Nature goes on,
does not depend on Man,
and yet how sad the voice
of the unseen savannah.

... and those that were not dead
were shot, the African
continued, in the head.
Birdsong grew loud and strong.

But surely those are words,
I thought; those monkey-cries
and birdcalls, those tree-sighs
are human syllables.

The uncontrollable
bird-chorus was of weeping:
the sound of inconsolable
humans weeping.

## *Heart Murmur*

Conditions in this body-shop
    or sweatshop, where I work,
    make me inclined to strike
and bring this unjust order to a stop.

All other organs get a break:
    the stomach rests from food,
    the brain sleeps, and the eyeball's hood
comes blinding down while I remain awake.

Eyes, mouth and eardrums know reward
    in colour, flavour, sound;
    the bowels' Underground
plays trains while I continue pumping blood.

The lungs enjoy sweet country air,
    the skin enjoys caress;
    the genitals' excess
of bliss exhausts me in my ribcage lair.

The brain co-ordinates and rules
    from high, dream-painted dome:
    my two-up, two-down home
is four corpuscle-crowded vestibules.

A wage, a day off at weekends,
    repair, some simple treats,
    respite from ceaseless beats,
and thanks, are not unreasonable demands.

And rest; rest would be best.
    It would be carnival.
    But, if I rest, our soul
would shut up shop and all our jobs be lost.

## *October Leafsong*

A whirr of sparrow-flight
    one fingertap of rain,
sounds that make air vibrate:
    the clatter of a train –

all suffice, when our time is come,
    to send us feathering down
to pattern paving stones
    with leafprints, cornflake brown.

        It is the time for Pax,
            surrender, fainites, barley:
        the Summer's gone, relax,
            leave hold, and go home early.

One fingertip of frost
    forges our gold-leaf guineas
whose value, at the most,
    is nothing; but such pennies

purchase the early dusk
    and deep blue violet sky
of lighting-up time; risk
    insolvency to buy

        long hibernation, rest,
            surrender, fainites, Pax;
        and winding-sheets of mist.
            It's long past equinox.

Resist! Let's dye our heads
    bright orange overnight:
but bottled blonde, and reds,
    only accelerate

decay. The pump has failed:
  sap-flow capitulates
to gravity. The world
    drags downward, into roots.

        So Pax, surrender, fainites,
          rain washes out our fire;
        fill gutters and block drainpipes,
          Death is our last desire.

## *Miss Jones*

The lady who cooks in the station carpark corner
is having a difficult morning. I hear from some distance
a screaming as though an over-excited macaw –
trained by more than commonly foulmouthed pirates
during long years at sea with never a sighting
of even so much as a female manatee –
were cursing the wintry skies of rainladen cloud.

Can the tenants of new low-cost redbrick
and minimal housing on the Paradise Project
have moved in already to lower the tone of the district?
I wonder, rounding the corner of Eden Road.
Would there be blood on the tarmac? But it's only Miss Jones
hurling hailstorms of crusts to her vermin hens,
(for "Somebody has to feed them"), shrieking meanwhile –
"Hideous smelly old woman, filthy old tart ..."
and words my pen is far too chaste to report.
Are you alright, Miss Jones? I ask as I pass her.
"Don't bother me now. Piss off. I have troubles enough,"
she shouts, and continues tirading. I walk to the station,
past her Ford in its shroud of tattered sheeting,
parked in the gutter, immobile outside number nine
where her parents died and deserted their blue-eyed daughter
to manage her life as best she could, and she failed
to pay the rent or the rates or the bills for heating
until she was, under protest, evicted. She swore
never to move away from her childhood's front-door.

So there she stays, tucked up in her tin-box motor,
cooking her camp-fire meals in the carpark corner,
hanging her washing to dry on the station gateway,
binding her chilblained feet in home-made sandals,
wearing serendipitous layers of clothing
and bringing down, by some thousands, property-prices.

When I return from the station, and re-cross the carpark,
she hails me as she carries her stew-bucket home
and asks if she was rude to me in the morning.
"Sometimes I must give vent to my feelings," she says
in ladylike accents, and I nod in answer.
"People get ill if they don't show their feelings"; she smiles
a six-year-old's gaptoothed smile, like a witchy child.
"We are warned against bearing false witness; we shouldn't pretend
so I let it all out," she explains. Yes, I understand.
Once she was somebody's cosseted blue-eyed girl
then suddenly she was a nobody, out in the cold
and telling her tale to the pigeons and stone-deaf sky;
unloading the hurt she suffered. I can understand –
and most of her old-time neighbours try to be kind.

For she is our lady of less than minimal housing,
she is our lady who bows to a living fire;
she is our lady of crusts for the oil-puddle pigeons
and she is our lady who binds up her swollen red feet
in cardboard, paper and tape; and she is our lady
who, when she can bear it no longer – our scarecrow lady –
flings her defiance and scorn at the swift grey sky
full of applauding wings.

## *Thomas de Quincey Down and Out in London*

Transient in homelessness:
scholar, orphan, gentle man;
Oxford Street, hard stepmother,
starved him, moved him on.

Crumbs that fell from bankrupt's table
scarcely fleshed his bones;
innocent street-walker Ann –
squandering her pence on wine –

saved his life alone.
Hand in hand down Swallow Street,
kiss in Golden Square,
catch the Mail and leave her weeping –

hopelessly, forever lost
and never found again.

# *Hölderlin's Last Night*

(7-6-1843 – after 30 years of insanity)

At my high tower window
on this summer night
I – who once was Poet –
cannot put a name
to that familiar stranger
with a shining face
who watches man's dark cradle.

I knew a lovely woman
in a former life
but now I don't remember
her name, or even mine.
That young man's words are spent,
and so I can't address
this silent visitant.

Can it be Death who looks
intently down at me?
A long-ago dead woman
would not remember me
and I can't name this disc
that shines so in the dusk
and floats across the dark.

I have no words to tame
such things; all things appear
naked of idea;
but this light falls like love –
lost storms of tenderness
rebounding from the walls
of time, now echo home.

## *The Sofa*

The couch she sat on, her upholstered nest
of layered cushions, folded blankets, duvets,
grew yearly as she piled on more and more
to make it high enough for her to rise
without a heave-ho from a strong-armed carer.
She spent her days beached on the coral reef
she and the years had made. She used to read,
she used to knit, she used to alter dresses
ordered from catalogues, or send them back.
She used to order care-ladies about,
and order meals on wheels, but seldom eat them.
She used to quell disorder in her Queendom –
her visible identity as Woman –
her packaging of wallpaper and curtains,
ornaments, and such stage-properties
as furnished her last bedsit.
Home was her mantra: My own home, My Home;
and, in a way, it was her work of art:
a collage, painting, stagelit rearrangement
of plywood, fablon, bright electric coals,
low lights and – lately – artificial flowers
which dropped no petals, needed no attention,
and neither did the cardboard cutout cat
in her shopwindow Home.

Past ninety, she clung on to what she knew
while moth gnawed at the pictured memory-cloak
tight folded in her skull.
It was as if the sphincters of her braincells
slackened and let the past escape.
Her days and weeks grew fugitive as smoke.
Twenty-three years of widowhood had vanished,
and all her homes combined to haunt the present,
as did her husband, Harry.

She thought he was upstairs, he had gone out;
"He's been gone several days. I'm getting worried."
"But Mum, Dad has been dead for twenty years."
She wept afresh for him.

We used to find her searching for lost things
left far behind in one of her past houses,
and she grew tired and cross with futile hunting,
sat down, dozed off, forgot about her losses,
also the blazing toast and boiling kettle.
Everything outside her dwindling world –
the market-place, its festivals, the shops,
buses to other towns, became a rumour:
less than a rumour since her deafness silenced
birdsong, engines growling, running taps,
the telephone, all voices, even her own,
down to the very spittle in her mouth.
The things that we who hear don't listen to
exploded through rejected hearing-aids.
Not natural, she said, though she wore glasses,
clothes, including corsets, perms, false teeth.
Reason was not her forté.
Unwittingly, she caused sore throats and migraines
among her neighbours, till they feared to visit
the moulting bower-bird who sat enthroned
in her dilapidated nest, forgetting
morning-callers by the afternoon.
Nobody's been. I haven't seen a soul.

Now we unmake her sofa, bag up cushions,
slabs of rubber, teastained blankets, duvets,
diversified with dogeared catalogues
and plastic bags, gritty with biscuit crumbs.
Such archaeology gives evidence
that time is not, as it may seem, a dream,
though when the time-processor wipes the tapes
of twenty, forty, eighty years, then childhood,

we doubt that anything at all has happened.
But here's time's proof. Dreams leave no residue,
while protozoa leave their tiny shells
to build, by death's long snowfall, seabed limestone;
and forests leave coal-measures; coral insects
leave us great reefs of coral, and this woman
built, through time, a sedimentary nest
that represents the years of her old age.
And, under its accretions, a hard sofa –
wartime utility, bought second-hand –
survives intact, and has a future life.
It goes to no museum, but will serve
a homeless family of immigrants
just setting up their future in this land.

## *Millennial Funerals*

1. ELIZABETH WINIFRED ROSE (1906 – 2000)

Ulysses, with his heart soaked through by the sea
and exhausted, must have worn the expression you wear:
you look as if, in a dream, you had swum the Channel,
the length of the Acton baths, or from shipwreck to shore.
You have swum the Styx, so that you lie breathless forever.
Having released your last gasp, your mouth remains open
letting your soul follow after. Relieved and triumphant,
you lie at last quite still on the pillowing sand.

What turbulent seas, what sharks, what hidden shoals
you have passed by more-or-less safely: two World Wars,
poverty, childbirth – protracted labour at home.
You saw two dawns while in throes, so "never no more."
One child was enough while tightrope-walking through life:
going out cleaning for one-and-sixpence a morning,
taking in lodgers, keeping things decent, and choosing –
now and again – a new hat or a trip to the seaside.

You have come through with honour, passed with honours
the utterly non-academic exam of life.
Even the vicar is saying nice things about you
though he has never seen you sat in a pew
or a box at the opera either. This vicar is new,
modern and tolerant. You might even have liked him
could you have met him before being packaged by death,
and had you not always suspected the Church of humbug.

"There's nothing up there," you used to declare with conviction,
pointing towards the ceiling, the flat upstairs,
but meaning the high blue ceiling above the world.
"There's something in here." You pressed both hands to your midriff,
implying both heart and soul and the tight-coiled spring

that kept you going since birth before the Great War:
from nineteen-o-six till the frightening three-nought number –
millennial year Two-thousand, but only just.

All of a sudden, the calm seas close to the shore
were breaking in suds on the beach, with an undertow
that washed you to and fro in forgotten time.
How you arrived wherever you were was unknown.
Middle-aged men were claiming to be your grandsons.
"Harry's gone out. It's been a very long day."
I felt a relief that matched the relief on your face
when your heart stopped beating, and death arrived as peace.

The bearers bow to your body. They trolley you out
into the snow-scented gale that snatches the wreaths
from your coffin and whirls them across the burial ground
so undertakers go chasing among the graves.
Your ghost might have smiled to see them at play like boys
and keeping your dark slot waiting. They lower you down.
Too chilled for emotion, we post you into the past
and say farewell.
           Then each of us carries you home.

2. NORMAN BLAMEY (1914 – 2000)

All through the tedious service that proved you were loved
by filling the church to capacity – standing-room only,
so even the porch overflowed – I could see your face
clear in my mind's eye, smiling with gentle humour.
I'm not a one to be haunted, but you were a friend
I was always delighted to see. I expect you were smiling
at most of your mourners, though mourning is not what I'd call it:
rather, a feeling of gratitude for having met you.

Born just in time for Christmas in Nineteen-fourteen –
the one the Great War was supposed to be over in time for –
marked, not by young men returning, but telegram-flocks

like flights of poisoned arrows shot home to roost
as permanent pain in the heart, and photographs
on mantel-shelves of front-parlours in sorrowing houses.
You first saw the light at the outset of four years of waste:
incomprehensible headlines and casualty lists.

At Somers Town School you fell in love with order:
fell in love with the orderly square-dance of numbers;
orderly lines of writing, the rules of grammar,
orderly forms of ritual, mystery's recipe:
order in painting, the mathematical masters:
della Francesca, Chardin, Morandi, Vermeer –
the last above all – were your heroes, but, in your twenties
you were caught up in the second instalment of chaos.

We never talked about that; but, one Christmas dinner,
sitting among the Academy students, you told me
about your childhood between the Regent's Canal
and acres of railway sidings, and soot-grimed stations –
Marylebone and St. Pancras, Euston, King's Cross
obliterating the Eighteenth Century fields.
The last rag of green was St. Pancras' burial ground
around the church where you, since your childhood, have worshipped.

You told me your painting was powered by the fear of failure
although it was really inspired by the great exemplars.
You said you never got over Royal College rejection.
Neither did I, I said, but you kept on painting,
and keeping on going is Nature's idea of success.
Your pictures hang in the Tate. Is that not enough?
"Nothing I've done seems important."
                              What more do you want?
"My fondest hope is of meeting my wife in Heaven."

## 3. JOSEF HERMAN (1911 – 2000)

Survivors, and middle-aged children of survivors,
intermingled with gentiles, sit shoulder to shoulder
in far too small a chapel to honour the artist
or even the mortal man, who endured much grief.
Some mourners are wearing yarmulkas; most are hatless
humanists who, in spite of the evidence,
believe in Man. Salt rivulets run down
strong faces, both for the many and the one.

Josef was gifted and lucky, he got away
after a hungry childhood in time of famine.
I know of the famine because my Quaker uncle
went with an ambulance unit to succour the starving
in Warsaw, after the war, in Nineteen-nineteen
when the artist, now dead in his box, was eight years old.
People dropped in the streets, and Josef remembered
the hunger that stunted his growth but not his ambition.

At children's morning tuppenny rushes, he first
encountered Art – in the fleapit cinema's flicks.
His favourite hero was Rin-Tin-Tin the Alsatian
dog. What a star! And slowly the realisation
dawned in his mind that films were not real but contrived
by plotting, cutting, construction: suspense and release
in death or survival. This was Rule One in the making
of artworks – a drama, or even a drawing or painting.

Somehow an artist discovers the knowledge he needs;
recognising his mentors, he feeds from their minds.
So Josef abandoned the Ghetto to seek for his kin,
and now he lies dead, being praised by eminent men,
in a coffin painted with sunflowers petalled with flame.
His granddaughters read out his words, with Josef's expression
haunting their immature features. Their father, his son,
announces the far-from-funereal Yiddisher music.

Discreetly, the flowery coffin glides into the furnace
while Josef is dancing like flames to the sound of trumpets,
peasant fiddles and timbrels, shouting and cymbals,
like King David dancing before the Lord.
Villages razed to the ground, lives gone up in smoke,
are celebrating a wedding. Slow mourners are leaving.
Music-possessed, among them, the five-year-old grandson
Josef is dancing for joy with all his might.

## *Filling in the Form*

This Spring, recording dates of season-signs
for climate watchers, I began too late
to catch the snowdrops, but the celandines –

shining, all uninvited, near my gate –
I registered, though bursting hawthorn buds
escaped my notice. Primroses, I caught,

likewise first bumblebees; of nesting birds –
the blackbird with a false moustache of hay.
By "Songthrush singing", for its triple words

I wrote "I wish", till suddenly, mid-May,
the garden filled with operatic pain.
From next-door's chimney-pipe, late in the day,

a sobbing primadonna poured a chain
of short soprano themes. Was this the last
of London's thrushes? Was her brood all slain?

She sang, like Niobe, of lives laid waste:
or so it seemed. She didn't come again,
though – in the main – the other wedding guests

turned up on time, near home. At Golders Green,
close by the station, my first swallow flew,
and beechleaves shone in the suburban scene.

I spotted, sunning on the grass at Kew,
a Comma spreading out twin treasure-maps
of capes and coves – her gypsy rags, brand new.

I saw another such burnt orange scrap
perched on the weathered planking of our fence.
A painted Peacock narrowly escaped

the flattening of its magnificence
beneath my tread as it soaked in the sun.
It fluttered up, warned by quick shadow-sense,

before being printed on a paving stone,
flat as a transfer. Drunkenly it flew
across the road to meet another one

around our appletree. No Holly Blue
arrived at all; but up and down our streets
conscripted forest stood in line and grew,

upheaving concrete slabs with restless roots.
It put out crumpled leaves: Horsechestnut, Birch
and Rowan feathers too. Small chorus parts

fill spaces. I hear distant Cuckoo speech.
Midmay, the crowning cross on Summer's dome
flies in. I see one first, then hear the screech

that says the Swifts reclaim their summer home –
our tainted sky – so Summer's stage is filled
with flying ballets – unseen insect-swarms –

the vast supporting cast hatched to be killed,
though all are remnants, merely, of the cloth
that interacted all about the world

before our kind built cities over Earth.
Here we preserve small Edens, sample weaves,
and I can sit in secret underneath

an Appletree now fully clothed in leaves
and green-bead fruit, prepared to read and sign
this form, in spotted shadow that deceives

my eyes so that the Speckled Wood's design,
with pearl-embroidered darkness on its wings,
almost succeeds in failing to be seen.

I rank it among Hopkins' "dappled things";
likewise the fledgeling Blackbirds, then address
and post my form off on its wanderings –

heavy with hints of threadbare sumptuousness.

## *The Angel*

I stayed in all day for the Angel
    who promised to call. He said – Wait:
so I dressed up demurely and waited
    but no angel perched on my gate.

I left doors and windows wide open
    so, whether on foot or in flight
on Miltonic wings, fanning fragrance,
    or if he was beamed down as light,

he shouldn't be able to miss me;
    his angelic greeting would bless,
his quivering wings would caress me,
    his fingers unbutton my dress.

But no angel came all the morning,
    only some twittering birds,
and no angel came before sundown
    though butterflies scribbled some words

in white and invisible writing,
    across empty air, to decode:
Don't idle there, passively waiting:
    Try the live lad down the road.

## *The Crimson Rose*

(for William Blake, 200 years later.)

Shamelessly beautiful,
    Rose you are well;
Unfurling your velvety
    Petals, you smell

Healthily sweet
    As you lift your red skirt,
Inviting the bees
    To your amorous heart.

## *Knocking On*

Past fifty, past that five-barred gate
    I shall not climb again,
my dazzled eyes appreciate
    the beauty of young men.

When I was in my upper teens
    and looked in young men's eyes
I saw, reflected in each lens,
    my beauty, shrunk in size

but full of power. I sensed the awe
    that fed my vanity
but when I too felt their desire
    my power drained from me.

Past seventy, I still revere
    the beauty of the young
but know that it must disappear
    like mine, before too long,

into a crumpled parchment bag
    with hair turned grey, or white;
and sight of pantaloon, or hag,
    kills Eros dead with fright.

So we are left with Agapé –
    let all the mirrors shiver –
look outward, active empathy
    translates the sensual fever:

but sometimes, still, the young men leap
    across dream's five-barred gate
and Eros frolics through my sleep –
    so late in life, so late!